songbirds

T0340437

Me

Topic songs for 4-7 year olds

Compiled and edited by
Ana Sanderson

With teaching notes by
Marie Tomlinson

and illustrations by
Kate Sheppard

Performed by
**Sandra Kerr, Ben Parry, Nancy Kerr,
James Fagan and Jane Sebba**

A&C BLACK • LONDON

First published 1997
A&C Black Publishers Ltd
Bloomsbury Publishing Plc
50 Bedford Square, London, WC1B 3DP
Reprinted 2005, 2008, 2011

Book and CD pack ISBN 978-0-7136-4800-3

SONGBIRDS: ME – book

Compiled and edited by Ana Sanderson
Teaching notes by Marie Tomlinson
Text © A&C Black
Cover artwork by Valentina Cavallini
Cover design by Fiona Grant
Line drawings by Kate Sheppard
Designed by Dorothy Moir
Printed by Halstan Printing Group, Amersham, Buckinghamshire

This book is produced using paper that is made from wood grown in
managed, sustainable forests. It is natural, renewable and recyclable.
The logging and manufacturing processes conform to the environmental
regulations of the country of origin.

SONGBIRDS: ME – recording

This recording was made without the aid of multi-tracking.
Songs and chants performed by Sandra Kerr and Ben Parry
Instrumental parts performed by:
     James Fagan (guitar, bouzouki, piano, clarinet, penny whistle, drum)
     Nancy Kerr (violin, mandolin, percussion)
     Sandra Kerr (concertina, guitar)
     Jane Sebba (bassoon, piano, percussion)
Recording engineered by John Whiting
Produced by Ana Sanderson. 68 minutes playing time

Also available – Songbirds: Seasons
A great collection of songs about spring, summer, autumn and winter,
growth and change, other climates and weather. The songs appeal especially
to young children and are short enough to teach by rote.
Book and CD pack.

Contents

Introduction

Songbirds: ME contains a wealth of old and new songs about the body, senses, food and drink, growth and change, and feelings. The songs in this collection have been chosen because:
• they will appeal to 4-7 year olds;
• their content and level of difficulty are appropriate for this age range;
• they can be easily related to topic and cross-curriculum work.

You do not need to be able to play a musical instrument or read music to use Songbirds: ME. It is a book and CD pack, giving you all you need to sing and enjoy these songs with children. You will find that:
• the words of each song are presented clearly in the book;
• the recording contains sung performances of all the songs to listen to, enjoy and learn from;
• instrument-only versions of the songs, suitable for accompanying your own performance in the classroom or at a concert, are also available on the recording;
• the notes – shown as letter names – of the first line of every song are given in the book and can be played on tuned percussion if required;
• there are suggestions on how to introduce, work on and improve your performance of the songs;
• melody lines with guitar chords can be found at the back of the book.

Singing in the classroom

More often than not, a singing child is a happy one! Young children love to explore their voices and also really enjoy participating in a song! These are both important activities for the development of their confidence, self-awareness and communication skills. There is also evidence to suggest that singing can aid learning to read and write. And, perhaps most importantly, the experience of singing is uplifting and feels good.

Posture is very important when singing. Although it is sometimes necessary to work on a song with children sitting on the floor, the resulting postures of the children – slumping, leaning or looking down at the floor – can lead to their breathing being constrained, and that in turn can cause poor singing. If possible, occasionally encourage the children to sit on chairs, or stand, when singing so that they can breathe more freely to improve their sound.

Sometimes, when focusing on breathing, children inhale excessively before singing, only to find that most of the air they have taken in is not useful. When considering breathing, encourage the children to breathe in time to sing – not too early or too late. Be aware that one should aim not to break up words, sentences or musical phrases with a breath at an inappropriate time, but to breathe at moments which do not interrupt the flow of the music or the sense of the words.

Help for teaching

With each song in this collection, there are suggestions of ways to introduce it to children or to improve their performance of it. Sometimes a performance can be improved simply by focusing on key words. There are other instances where the children are encouraged to work on the quality of a vowel or consonant featured in words of a song.

One of the preliminary activities sometimes suggested for introducing a song is that the recording is played to the children and they are encouraged to join in with particular words or lines. This helps develop the children's listening and appraising skills as well as their singing skills – and is an excellent way of giving the children the opportunity to absorb a song. Much valuable work can be done on a few lines before children are ready to perform a whole song.

There are songs for which children can make up their own words or suggestions to incorporate into the song. When asking children for their ideas, make suggestions of your own so that they become familiar with the process of thinking of and contributing ideas. The children can sing new verses with their words with the instrument-only accompaniment tracks.

Many of the songs in this collection contain actions. Young children often find it difficult to sing and perform an action at the same time. It is advisable to practise them separately at first.

Occasionally there are suggestions for incorporating tuned percussion into your teaching or a performance. For this, chime bars, glockenspiels or xylophones are appropriate.

At least two teaching points are given with each song – beginning with the easiest and progressing to the more difficult. When you go back to a song, perhaps a day, a week, a month or even a year after introducing it, you can focus on the teaching suggestions to help improve your children's performance. Though this collection is intended for 4-7 year olds, inevitably there are some songs which are more appropriate for the younger and older extremes. However there is plenty of potential for developing an individual performance of a song which is appropriate for your children. Your children may enjoy going back to a simple song to develop and improve their performance of it.

The recording

There are two versions of each item in this book on the recording: a sung performance with instruments and voices and an instrument-only version suitable for accompanying your own performance. The songs have been recorded at speeds suitable for young children to sing along with. The instruments played are all acoustic – there are no synthesized sounds.

There is an instrumental introduction to each song with which you will need to be familiar before singing along with the accompaniment track. Listen to the sung version of a song first and sing along with it a few times. When you know how it goes and know when to begin singing, try singing along with the accompaniment track.

(Note that the accompaniment tracks of the call and responses 3 Kye Kye Kule and 23 Mahachagogo contain the leader's part. The accompaniment track of 13 Food wrap contains a guide vocal. The short rhyme 15 Growing is repeated on the accompaniment track.)

Finally, and most importantly, **Songbirds: ME** is a wonderful collection of songs – we very much hope you and your children enjoy singing them!

1 Doctor Knickerbocker

Doctor Knickerbocker, Knickerbocker number nine,
He likes to dance and keep in time.
Now I've got the rhythm in my **head**,
    (Nod nod)
Now I've got the rhythm in my head,
    (Nod nod)
Now I've got the rhythm of the number nine.
One ... two ... three four five six seven eight nine!

Doctor Knickerbocker, Knickerbocker number nine,
He likes to dance and keep in time.
Now I've got the rhythm in my **hands**,
    (Clap clap)
Now I've got the rhythm in my hands,
    (Clap clap)
Now I've got the rhythm of the number nine.
One ... two ... three four five six seven eight nine!

... Now I've got the rhythm in my knees,
   (Knock knock) ...

... Now I've got the rhythm in my feet,
   (Stamp stamp) ...

Ask the children to listen to the recording of the song while performing the actions suggested in each verse. Perform them where indicated. Make the actions tidy (particularly the nods of the first verse) and in time with the music. If the children find the knee knocks or feet stamps difficult, try tapping knees or feet with hands instead.

The numbers *one* to *nine* are spoken. Practise them by chanting the first five numbers, leaving a short wait after *one* and *two*:

   One (wait) two (wait) three four five ...

When the children can confidently chant the numbers, perform the actions with them. Remember that the spoken numbers lead straight into the following verse – except for the last verse.

When the children can confidently sing the song, think of other parts of the body and appropriate actions for new verses, eg fingers and clicks, elbows and flaps. Then ask the children to make their own suggestions for new verses.

A♯ A♯ B B G G G G E D G G G
Doc-tor Knick-er-bock-er, Knick-er-bock-er, num-ber nine

Traditional, adapted by Jane Sebba

2 Head shoulders baby

Head shoulders baby
   One *(clap)* two *(clap)* three.
Head shoulders baby
   One *(clap)* two *(clap)* three.
Head shoulders head shoulders,
Head shoulders baby
   One *(clap)* two *(clap)* three.

Hands fingers baby
   One *(clap)* two *(clap)* three.
Hands fingers baby
   One *(clap)* two *(clap)* three.
Hands fingers hands fingers,
Hands fingers baby
   One *(clap)* two *(clap)* three.

Hips tummy baby
   One *(clap)* two *(clap)* three ...

Knees ankles baby
   One *(clap)* two *(clap)* three ...

The actions of this song make it a challenging one to perform. Build up your performance gradually. First learn the words of each verse. Then practise touching the parts of the body each time they are mentioned. (Note that the third verse *hips tummy* is the easiest as the actions hinder the singing least.)

The numbers *one, two* and *three* are sung on the note **F**. If you wish, you can ask a child to join in playing this note on a chime bar whenever these words are sung.

Make up new verses with other parts of the body, eg nose and forehead, chest and elbow. Then ask the children to find partners and make up their own verses.

When the children are confident with the song, ask them to clap where indicated, in time with the music.

G♯   A   F   D   C   F   F   F
Head shoul-ders ba-by one *(clap)* **two** *(clap)* **three**

Traditional American

3 Kye kye kule

Leader:

Kye kye kule.

Kye kye kofi nsa.

Kofi nsa langa.

Kaka shi langa.

Kum adende.

Children:

Kye kye kule.

Kye kye kofi nsa.

Kofi nsa langa.

Kaka shi langa.

Kum adende.

All:
Kum adende.
Hey!

Pronunciation guide:
Kye – chay
Kule – koo-lay
Kofi nsa – ko-feen-sa
Langa – lahn-gah
Kaka shi – kah-kah shee
Kum – koom
Adende – ah-den-day

The words of this very popular action song come from several dialects and cannot be translated specifically. The leader performs each line with actions and everyone else copies and echoes.

First practise chanting the words. Then sing the words. When the words of the song are secure, add these actions to your performance:
Kye kye kule – pat head four times;
Kye kye kofi nsa – pat shoulders four times, twisting the top half of the body from side to side;
Kofi nsa langa – put hands on waist, again twisting the top half of the body from side to side;
Kaka shi langa – tap knees four times;
Kum adende – touch ankles on *kum* and waist on *adende*;
Hey – throw hands up in the air.

(Note that the accompaniment track of this song on the recording contains the leader's part for the children to echo.)

G   G   F G
Kye kye ku-le

Traditional Akan

4 You need skin

You need skin,
So take good care of it,
Don't harm a hair of it,
What would you do without it?
Keep it clean,
Soapy water every day
Will wash the dirt and smells away,
'Cause you need skin.

Whether you're fat or whether you're thin,
It stops the germs from crawling in;
Whether you're skinny or whether you're stout,
It keeps the blood from trickling out.
    You need skin ...

Whether you're black or whether you're brown,
It keeps your tummy from tumbling out;
Whether you're silly or whether you're smart,
It stops your bones from falling apart.
    You need skin ...

The body

Whether you're dark or whether you're fair,
Skin's the thing for growing hair;
It's waterproof in rainy weather,
And keeps the bits of your body together.
    You need skin ...

Play the recording of the song. Focus on the chorus and listen for the words *you need skin* and *keep it clean*. Both have the same tune. Encourage the children to listen and join in with these lines. Through listening, they will become familiar with the rest of the chorus.

When the children are familiar with the chorus, learn the verses. The children may need to practise the words slowly at first in order to articulate them clearly.

Sing the 'w' of *whether* strongly, moving the lips with energy. Take a good breath before the last line of each verse in order to be ready to make a long sound on the last word:

    v1 – *out___*
    v2 – *(a)-part___*
    v3 – *(to-ge)-ther___*

A   F♯   D
You need skin

Words and music by Leon Rosselson

5 Hair

Hair can be short, hair can be long,
It can be fine or thick and strong.
It can be curly, framing your face,
It can be smooth, or all over the place.
  Hair grows slowly, takes its time,
  Takes its time, takes its time.
  Hair grows slowly, takes its time.
  You can never rush it,
  No matter how you brush it.

Hair can be yellow, hair can be brown,
Tied up in bunches, or hanging straight down.
Hair can be black, or hair can be red,
Curled into ringlets all over your head.
  Hair grows slowly, takes its time ...

Tie it in ribbons, tie it in bows,
Cut it off short and wait till it grows.
Wear it in dreadlocks, wear it in plaits,
Or cover it over in different hats.
  Hair grows slowly, takes its time ...

The body

Hair can be short, hair can be long,
It can be fine or thick and strong.
It can be curly, framing your face,
It can be smooth, or all over the place.

Begin by learning the chorus. Encourage the children to listen to the recording and to join in with the first three lines of the chorus. Make these lines smooth when you sing them and sustain the word *time* whenever it is sung. Through listening to the rest of the song, the children will become familiar with the end of the chorus and the verses.

Focus on the verses. Practise the words slowly at first, in order that the children hear them and articulate them clearly.

Sing the words of the verses with a bounce to contrast with the chorus. Improve your performance by making good, sustained vowel sounds on the rhyming words at the end of each line:

    v1 – *long, strong;*
          face, place;
    v2 – *brown, down;*
          red, head;
    v3 – *bows, grows;*
          plaits, hats.

F♯ F♮ F♯ D
Hair can be short

Words and music by Jill Darby

The body

6 Uncle Tom

Uncle Tom had a chest, chest, chest,
Uncle Tom had a chest, chest, chest,
Uncle Tom had a chest, chest, chest,
He gave it to his niece, niece, niece.
    Thumbs up Uncle Tom,
    Thumbs up Uncle Tom,
    Thumbs up Uncle Tom,
    Give him a great big clap. *(clap clap)*

Uncle (ankle)   Tom (tum)

chest

There's a **necklace** in the chest, chest, chest,
There's a necklace in the chest, chest, chest,
There's a necklace in the chest, chest, chest,
That Tom gave to his niece, niece, niece.
    Thumbs up Uncle Tom,
    Thumbs up Uncle Tom,
    Thumbs up Uncle Tom,
    Give him a great big clap. *(clap clap)*

niece (knees)

Thumbs up

There's a wristwatch in the chest, chest, chest ...
Thumbs up Uncle Tom ...

There's a headscarf in the chest, chest, chest ...
Thumbs up Uncle Tom ...

Older children will particularly enjoy this challenging song.

Encourage children to join in with the chorus and to smile on the words *Thumbs up Uncle Tom*. When they can confidently sing the words, add these actions:
Thumbs up – put thumbs up in the air;
Uncle – touch ankle;
Tom – touch tummy.
Clap twice at the end of the chorus, in time with the music.

Learn the verses. When the children can sing them securely, add any of these actions:
Uncle – touch ankle;
Tom – touch tummy;
Chest – touch chest;
Niece – touch knees;
Necklace – touch neck;
Wristwatch – touch wrist and eyes;
Headscarf – touch head and neck.

Make up your own verses with suitable actions using any of these suggestions: bum bag, waistcoat, shoulder pad, hip flask, knee sock, toothbrush.

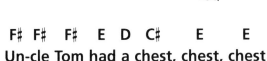

F# F# F# E D C# E E
Un-cle Tom had a chest, chest, chest

Words and music by Jan Holdstock

The body

7 Bones

You've got to have bones to *(clap)*
Hang your body on,
Got to have bones to *(clap)*
Hang your body on,
Got to have bones to hang your body on,
    That's what bones are for.
If you didn't have bones to *(clap)*
Hang your body on,
Didn't have bones to *(clap)*
Hang your body on,
Didn't have bones to hang your body on,
    You'd be a big blob of jelly on the floor!

Begin by teaching the song without the claps. When the children can sing it confidently, add the claps. Notice that the third time each of the lines *got to have bones to* and *didn't have bones to* are sung, there are no claps afterwards.

Work the lips on the 'b' sound of *body, bone* and *big blob*.

The words of the lines *got to have bones to* and *didn't have bones to* are all sung on the note **G**. Ask a child to join in playing the rhythm of those words on a chime bar **G**.

D   G   G   G   G   G
You've got to have bones to

Words and music by Kaye Umanksy

8 Body sense

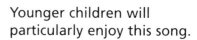

I spy with my little eye,

I hear with my little ear.

A smell goes up my nose,

And I taste with my tongue which I hide in here,

I taste with my tongue in here.

But I can feel all over

The whole of my body,

I can feel all over:

I can feel on my head,

I can feel on my nose;

I can feel with my fingers

And my toes.

E G E A G G E
I spy with my lit-tle eye

Younger children will particularly enjoy this song.

Talk about the parts of the body featured in the song – *eye, ear, nose* and *tongue* (which are nearer together) and *head, nose, fingers* and *toes* (which are further apart). Ask the children to point to them as they listen to the recording.

Work on the 'ee' sound of *feel*. Smile, with eyebrows high, in order to encourage a good 'ee' sound.

When the children are confident of the words of the song, ask them to point to the parts of the body as they sing about them.

Words and music by Ana Sanderson

9 What can you see?

What can you see? What can you see?
I can see the pattern of the waves on the sea.

What can you hear? What can you hear?
I can hear the seagulls when they're flying near.

What can you smell? What can you smell?
I can smell the salt that's hiding in a shell.

What can you feel? What can you feel?
I can feel the stones moving under my heel.

What can you taste? What can you taste?
I can taste my ice-cream, couldn't bear to let it waste.

This song is good for miming what you can see, hear, smell, touch and taste. The children can invent mimes for each verse and perform them as they listen to the recording of the song.

Perform this song as a question and answer. Divide the class into two groups; one sings the first line of each verse (the question) and the other sings the second line (the answer).

Encourage the children to sing the words smoothly. Make the words *see, hear, smell, feel* and *taste* long sounds.

G G A G G G A G
What can you see? What can you see?

Words and music by Sue Nicholls

10 Here's a quiz

Sniff, sniff, here's a little quiz,
Can you say what this **smell** is?
(Pause for a sniff)
Sniff, sniff, yes I can
I think it's **flowers**,
That's what that smell is.

Listen, listen, here's a little quiz,
Can you say what this **sound** is?
(Pause for a listen)
Listen, listen, yes I can,
I think it's **wrapping paper**,
That's what that smell is.

Munch, munch, here's a little quiz,
Can you say what this **taste** is?
(Pause for a munch)
Munch, munch, yes I can,
I think it's **sandwiches**,
That's what that taste is.

Younger children will particularly enjoy this song.

Talk about the senses of smell, hearing and taste. Practise sniffing, listening and pretending to munch – all of which exercise the muscles around the lips. This will help with making the words of the song sound clearer.

Encourage the children to make up their own versions of this song. Ask them to list things which have scent, can be heard, or have taste. Incorporate the children's ideas into the song.

In the middle of each verse, there is a pause to sniff, to listen, or to munch. The children may wish to make sound effects during these pauses. In the first and third verses, the sound effects will probably suggest the actions of sniffing and munching. For the second verse, the children may be able to develop sound effects suggesting what they are hearing.

A   F#   A   B A G F#
Sniff, sniff, here's a lit-tle quiz

Words and music by Jane Sebba

Food and drink

11 Sweet potato

Soon as we all bake **sweet potatoes**,
Sweet potatoes, sweet potatoes,
Soon as we all bake sweet potatoes;
    Eat them up right quick.

Soon as we all bake **tasty pizzas** ...

Soon as we all bake **crunchy biscuits** ...

Soon as supper's done, Mummy hollers,
Mummy hollers, Mummy hollers,
Soon as supper's done, Mummy hollers;
    Time to go to bed.

Ask the children to think of foods they could make or bake and add them to the song, eg chocolate pudding, ripe bananas, apple crumble, red tomatoes, soggy porridge, toast and butter.

The food words *sweet potatoes, tasty pizza* and so on are all sung on the note **C**. Ask a child to play a chime bar **C** to the rhythm of the food words whenever they are sung.

Encourage the children to make a good 'oo' sound whenever they sing the word *soon*. Listen to the recording of this song to hear a good example sound.

C' A Bb A F   C   C C C
Soon as we all bake sweet po-ta-toes

Traditional, with words adapted by
Ana Sanderson

12 I'm so hot

I'm so hot, it's no joke.
I could drink a whole can of Coke.

I'm so hot, even in the shade.
I would love a litre of lemonade.

I'm so hot, I should think
I need a bucket of pink, fizzy drink.

I'm so hot, think I oughta
Be able to finish up a bath full of water.

I'm so hot, I could take
A swimming pool full of vanilla milk-shake.

I'm so hot, I have a notion
I could swallow the Atlantic Ocean.

Play the recording of this song and ask the children to join in singing the words *I'm so hot*.

Practise chanting this sequence: *can, litre, bucket, bath, swimming pool, Atlantic Ocean.* Chant it quietly, then loudly. Then start quietly, getting gradually louder. (Avoid *Atlantic Ocean* becoming extremely loud.) When singing the song, reflect the increasing volume of drinks by starting the song quietly, getting gradually louder throughout.

C E C E G E
I'm so hot, it's no joke

Words and music by David Moses

13 Food wrap

We are hungry, tummies are rumbly,
Let's raid the kitchen, who's going to cook?

I will, you will, we will, who will?
What's in the fridge? Let's have a look.

(Rub tummies)
Mmmmmmmmmmmm

I want chocolate!   *(Clap)* Why not?
I want lentils!   *(Clap)* Why not?
I want peaches!   *(Clap)* Why not?
We'll be sick if we eat that lot!

Chop it up, stir it up, put it in the pot,
Stick it in the oven till it's piping hot.

(Rub tummies)
Mmmmmmmmmmmm

I want ice cream!   *(Clap)* Not hot.
I want curry!   *(Clap)* Quite hot.
I want chillies!   *(Clap)* Very hot.
Are we really going to eat that lot?

Food and drink

Chop it up, stir it up, put it in the pot,
Stick it in the oven till it's piping hot.

(Rub tummies)
Mmmmmmmmmmmmm

(Starting quietly, getting louder and faster)
I want chips and walnut whips and
eggs and ham and strawberry jam and
mushy peas and melted cheese
    and a packet of crisps –
CERTAINLY NOT!

(Slowly, as though with a tummy ache)
(Clap) Guess what?
Can you spot what *(clap)* we've got?

(Even slower, as if feeling sick)
We are feeling very very ...
(Quickly, as if feeling better)
Hungry, hungry, tummies are rumbly,
Let's raid the kitchen, who's going to cook?

Young children will enjoy listening to the recording of this rap and joining in at the right moments with *Mmmmmmmm*. As they listen out for when to join in, they will be absorbing the whole rap for the future.

Focus on the 'w' sounds of *I will, you will, we will, who will* in the first section, and the 'p' sounds of *put it in the pot* and *piping hot*. Make the 'w' and 'p' sounds clear.

Divide the children into three groups: one to perform the first section, another for the second, and so on. All the children can perform the last section. If you wish, you can choose soloists to perform particular lines.

This rap can be performed unaccompanied or with the accompaniment track which contains a guide vocal.

Rap by Jane Sebba

Food and drink

14 Jelly belly

Two, four, six, eight,
Tell me what is on your plate:
    Jelly!
We're going to have some jelly,
    Hurrah, hurrah!
We're going to have some jelly,
    Hurrah, hurrah!
Jelly for your dinner,
Jelly for your tea,
Jelly, jelly down your belly,
Hip hip hip hurrah!

Two, four, six, eight,
Tell me what is on your plate:
    Ice-cream!
We're going to have some ice-cream,
    Hurrah, hurrah!
We're going to have some ice-cream,
    Hurrah, hurrah!
Ice-cream for your dinner,
Ice-cream for your tea,
Ice-cream, jelly down your belly,
Hip hip hip hurrah!

Two, four, six, eight,
Tell me what is on your plate:
Beans!
We're going to have some beans,
Hurrah, hurrah!
We're going to have some beans,
Hurrah, hurrah!
Beans for your dinner,
Beans for your tea,
Beans, ice-cream, jelly down your belly,
Hip hip hip hurrah!

Two, four, six, eight,
Tell me what is on your plate:
Pickled onions ...

Everyone will enjoy joining in with the first two lines which are chanted. This song gives children the opportunity both to sing and to speak.

Focus on *hip* and *hurrah*. Avoid allowing these words to sound lazy – make each 'h' energetic. Sing the last line of each verse with gusto but avoid shouting.

This is a cumulative song – all the foods mentioned are listed in reverse order in the second last line of each verse. Continue adding your own verses, asking the children to suggest whatever foods they would like to add, and fitting those words into the tune.

G   C   C   C   E   G G
We're going to have some jel-ly

Adapted from traditional by P. Trezise

Growth and change

15 Growing

Flowers grow like this;

Trees grow like this;

I grow

Just like that!

Perform the actions suggested by the words of this short rhyme. Discuss with the children how their movements grow in size as the rhyme progresses.

The sound of the children's voices can grow as they perform the rhyme. First explore how sound can grow. Choose one line of the rhyme. Ask a small number of children to say it, then repeat it adding more children until everyone is saying it. Then explore performing the whole rhyme, beginning very quietly, ending loudly.

This rhyme is best performed either unaccompanied or with your own accompaniment. You can invite children to choose percussion instruments with which they would like to accompany their performance.

(Note that the accompaniment track on the recording is a repeat of the vocal track.)

Traditional

16 Too big for my boots

I've grown too big for my **boots**,
(Stamp stamp)
Oh dear,
They don't fit my feet like they did last year.
Oh, they fitted me in the shop,
Now they pinch my toes on top.
Of my feet I must take care,
I've only got one pair,
    So I'd better get another,
    Better get another,
    Better get another pair of boots to wear.

I've grown too big for my **trainers** ...

I've grown too big for my **shoes** ...

Focus on the last three lines of the verse so I'd better get another ... pair of boots to wear. Explore these words with the children by speaking them, whispering them, shouting them and singing them.

When the children are familiar with the song, ask them to suggest various movements they might make in different types of footwear, eg stamping in boots, kicking a football in trainers, walking in shoes. Encourage them to perform their actions neatly after the first line of each verse.

Ask the children to suggest types of footwear, eg wellies, sandals, flip-flops, slippers, clogs. Make up new verses with the suggestions.

C   D   E   F   A   A   F
I've grown too big for my boots

Words and music by Ana Sanderson

17 Going over the sea

When I was one I had some fun,
The day I went to sea.
I jumped aboard a sailing ship,
And the captain said to me:
'I'm going this way, that way,
Forwards and backwards,
Over the deep, blue sea.
A bottle of rum to fill my tum,
That's the life for me.'

When I was two I buckled my shoe ...

When I was three I grazed my knee ...

When I was four I shut the door ...

When I was five I learned to dive ...

When I was six I picked up sticks ...

When I was seven I went to Devon ...

When the children can confidently perform this song, add some actions:
One – hold up one finger;
Jumped – jump;
This way – place left hand over left eyebrow, (as if looking into the distance);
That way – place right hand over right eyebrow;
Forwards – lean forwards;
Backwards – lean back.
If you wish, divide the children into two groups – one to sing and one to perform the actions.

I'm going at the beginning of the fifth line of each verse is drawn out. Be sure to take a good breath (not too much) before this line.

If you wish, extend the song with three more verses:
When I was eight I learned to skate;
When I was nine I climbed a vine;
When I was ten I caught a hen.
Then encourage the children to invent their own verses, using rhyming, to develop their own rhyming skills.

C   F   F   F A C' A F
When I was one I ate a bun

Traditional, adapted by Ana Sanderson

18 All I want for Christmas
(is my two front teeth)

All I want for Christmas is my two front teeth,
My two teeth, see my two front teeth!
Gee, if I could only have my two front teeth,
Then I could wish you 'Merry Christmas.'
    It seems so long since I could say,
    'Sister Susie sitting on a thistle!'
    Gosh, oh gee, how happy I'd be,
    If I could only whistle ... *(thhh)*
All I want for Christmas is my two front teeth,
My two front teeth, see my two front teeth!
Gee, if I could only have my two front teeth,
Then I could wish you 'Merry Christmas!'

Listen to the recording of the song with the children and count how many times they hear the words *two front teeth*. (They occur eight times.)

The words *two front teeth* are sung on different notes each time. Using tuned percussion, try playing the *two front teeth* melody notes. Here they are in the order they come in the song:

F♯ D D   F D D
two front teeth   two front teeth

E C C   F♯ D D
two front teeth   two front teeth

F♯ D D   F D D
two front teeth   two front teeth

E C C   F G A
two front teeth   two front teeth

Try singing the various tunes.

When the children are familiar with the song, encourage the children to smile when they sing the words *two front teeth*.

G F♯ G F♯ G A G E F♯ D D
All I want for Christ-mas is my two front teeth

Words and music by Don Gardner

19 I love to laugh

I love to laugh,
Ha! Ha! Ha! Ha!
Loud and long and clear.
I love to laugh,
Ho! Ho! Ho! Ho!
It's getting worse ev'ry year.
The more I laugh,
Ha! Ha! Ha! Ha!
The more I fill with glee
And the more the glee,
Hee! Hee! Hee! Hee!
The more I'm a merrier
Me! Ha! Ha!
Me! Ho! Ho!
Me! It's embarrassing!
The more I'm a merrier me!

We love to laugh,
Ha! Ha! Ha! Ha!
Loud and long and clear.
We love to laugh,
Ho! Ho! Ho! Ho!
So ev'rybody can hear.
The more you laugh,
Ha! Ha! Ha! Ha!
The more you fill with glee
And the more the glee,
Hee! Hee! Hee! Hee!
The more we're a merrier
We! Ha! Ha!
We! Ho! Ho!
We! It's embarrassing!
The more we're a merrier we!

Work on producing good vowel sounds for *ha, ho* and *hee*. Start each of these words with a good 'h' sound.

Both verses include several words containing an 'ee' sound: *glee, hee, me* and *we*. To make a good 'ee' sound, smile as you sing.

Focus on making a good 'l' sound for *love, laugh* and *long*. Use the 'l' to launch the words clearly.

G A F C'
I love to laugh

(from Mary Poppins)
Words and music by Richard M Sherman and Robert B Sherman

20 Very, very sad

I lost my book and I'm very, very sad,
Very, very sad, very, very sad.
I know I put it down when my friend came round,
Now I haven't got a book and I'm oh so sad.

I lost my teddy and I'm very, very sad,
Very, very sad, very, very sad.
I made an awful fuss 'cause I left it on the bus
Now I haven't got a teddy and I'm oh so sad.

I lost my friend and I'm very, very sad,
Very, very sad, very, very sad.
My friend's gone away on a long holiday,
Now I haven't got a friend and I'm oh so sad.

I lost my cat and I'm very, very sad,
Very, very sad, very, very sad,
I wonder why all creatures have to die,
Now I haven't got a cat and I'm oh so sad.

This song is a good one for children to show sadness in the way they sing the words and tune.

Before teaching this song to children, you may wish to discuss the experience of loss of toys, friends and pets with them.

Encourage the children to sing the tune smoothly. Gently emphasize each 'v' for *very* and each 's' for *sad*.

G F♯ E   E   E   E   F♯ G F♯ G E F♯
I__ lost my book and I'm ve-ry, ve-ry sad

Words and music by David Moses

21 Doctor, Doctor

Doctor, Doctor, help me do,
I feel a little sick and I don't want to.
Give me a powder, give me a pill.
Hurry, hurry Doctor, 'cause I do feel ill.

Nurse, Nurse, help me please,
I've got a little cough, I've got a little sneeze.
I got wet through, I think I caught a chill.
Hurry, hurry Nurse, 'cause I do feel ill.

Please Mister Dentist, don't hang about,
I ate too many sweets and my teeth are dropping out.
Give them a polish with your high speed drill.
Hurry Mister Dentist, 'cause I do feel ill.

This song has a simple melody that younger children will particularly enjoy.

In the first line, focus on the 'd' of *Doctor* and *do*; in the third line, use the 'g' of *give* and the 'p' of *powder* and *pill*. Use these sounds to launch the words clearly.

The tunes of the first and third lines consist of two notes: F♯ and D. When the children are familiar with the song, give them opportunities to work out how to play the tunes on two chime bars. A child can join in playing the tune of these lines during a performance.

F♯ F♯ D D F♯ F♯ D
Doc-tor, Doc-tor, help me do

Words and music by David Moses

 **Feelings**

22 Me? I'm great!

Wonderful, marvellous,
I am quite magnificent!
Excellent in every way,
Brilliant is what I say!
First-class, A-1, top-notch, well done,
Let me tell you straight:
Wonderful, marvellous,
    Me? I'm great!

This is an excellent song for singing with enthusiasm. Encourage the children to launch the first word *wonderful* by emphasizing the first syllable with a good 'w'. Ask the children to make their faces like elastic to produce well the three syllables of *marvellous*.

Throughout the song, the children should have bright eyes and smiling mouths to convey the spirit of the words!

Make the last line extra effective by ensuring that there is a silence between *me?* and *I'm great*. This will help to round off the song with style.

D   A, A,   F♯ D   D
Wond-er-ful, mar-vel-lous

Words and music by Jane Sebba

23 Mahachagogo

Leader:	Children:
Mahachagogo says:	
Mmmm.	
	Mmmm.
Aaaah.	
	Aaaah.
Oooh.	
	Oooh.
Lah lah lah.	
	Lah lah lah.
Then he stops.	
	Then he stops.
Why?	
	I don't know.

Nor do I.
But I do know that when he feels **cold**,
Mahachagogo says:
(Repeat chant in manner of the mood or feeling.)

Leader, to finish:
But I do know that when he feels **tired**,
Mahachagogo says no more.

This is a simple echo chant in which children can explore different emotions. Try it with you leading and the children copying. Make sure that when you reach the question *why?* the children do not copy you, but answer the question with *I don't know.*

Try different moods and emotions, such as angry, quiet, frightened, serious, playful, sorry and so on.

(Note that the accompanying track on the recording contains the leader's part only which you can use as an alternative to leading the chant yourself.)

When the children know the chant well, invite a confident child to be the leader.

Chant by Ana Sanderson

Melody lines

1 Doctor Knickerbocker

Traditional, adapted by Jane Sebba

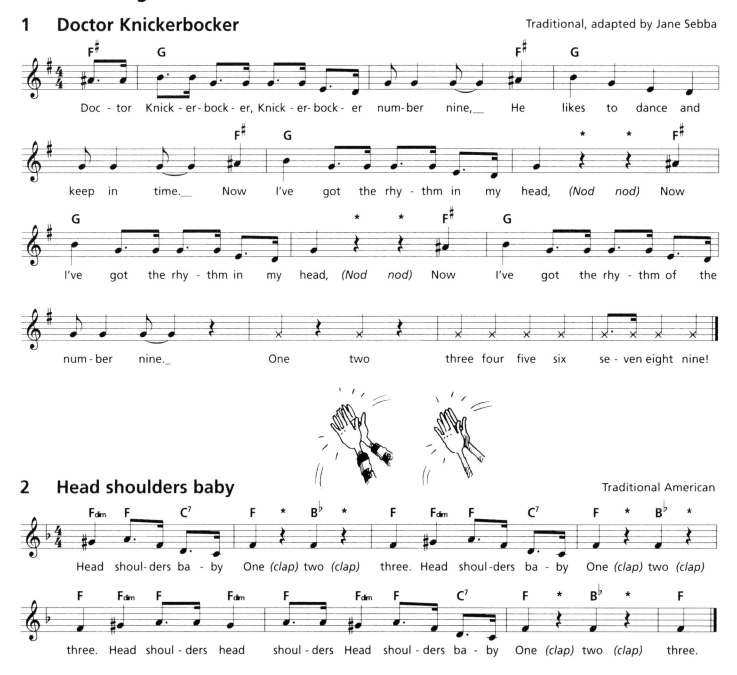

Doc - tor Knick - er - bock - er, Knick - er - bock - er num - ber nine,__ He likes to dance and keep in time.__ Now I've got the rhy - thm in my head, *(Nod nod)* Now I've got the rhy - thm in my head, *(Nod nod)* Now I've got the rhy - thm of the num - ber nine.__ One two three four five six se - ven eight nine!

2 Head shoulders baby

Traditional American

Head shoul - ders ba - by One *(clap)* two *(clap)* three. Head shoul - ders ba - by One *(clap)* two *(clap)* three. Head shoul - ders head shoul - ders Head shoul - ders ba - by One *(clap)* two *(clap)* three.

3 Kye kye kule

Traditional Akan

C

1 Kye kye ku - le.   2 Kye kye ku - le.   1 Kye kye ko - fi nsa.   2 Kye kye ko - fi nsa.
(Chay chay koo - lay)   (Chay chay ko - feen - sah)

1 Ko - fi nsa lan - ga.   2 Ko - fi nsa lan - ga.   1 Ka - ka shi lan - ga.   2 Ka - ka shi lan - ga.
(Ko - fee sah - lahn - gah)   (Kah - kah shee lahn - gah)

1 Kum   a - den - de.   2 Kum   a - den - de. 1+2 Kum   a - den - de.   Hey!
(Koom   ah - den - day)

4 You need skin

Words and music by Leon Rosselson

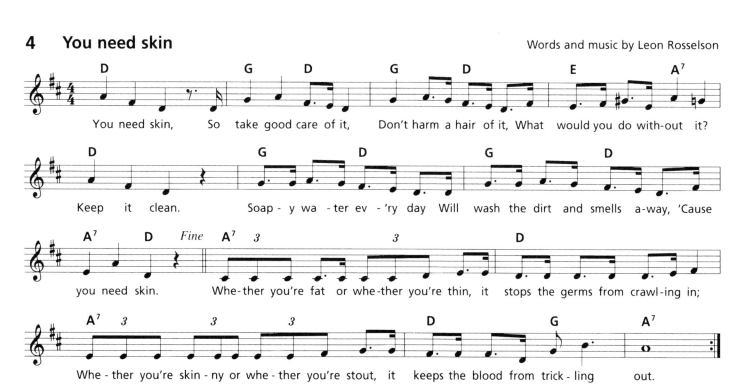

D   **G** **D**   **G** **D**   **E**   **A⁷**

You need skin,   So take good care of it,   Don't harm a hair of it, What would you do with-out it?

D   **G** **D**   **G**   **D**

Keep   it clean.   Soap - y wa - ter ev - 'ry day Will wash the dirt and smells a - way, 'Cause

A⁷ **D** *Fine* **A⁷** *3*   *3*   **D**

you need skin.   Whe - ther you're fat or whe - ther you're thin, it   stops the germs from crawl - ing in;

A⁷ *3*   *3*   *3*   **D**   **G**   **A⁷**

Whe - ther you're skin - ny or whe - ther you're stout, it   keeps the blood from trick - ling   out.

5 Hair

Words and music by Jill Darby

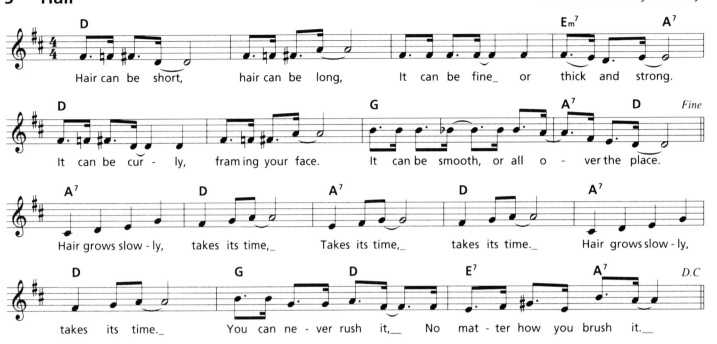

Hair can be short, hair can be long, It can be fine_ or thick and strong.

It can be cur - ly, fram ing your face. It can be smooth, or all o - ver the place.

Hair grows slow - ly, takes its time,_ Takes its time,_ takes its time._ Hair grows slow - ly,

takes its time._ You can ne - ver rush it,_ No mat - ter how you brush it.__

6 Uncle Tom

Words and music by Jan Holdstock

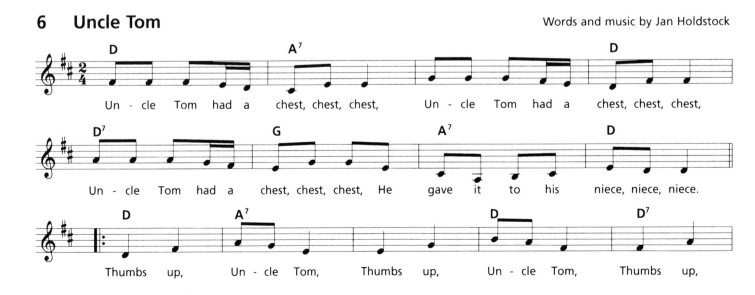

Un - cle Tom had a chest, chest, chest, Un - cle Tom had a chest, chest, chest,

Un - cle Tom had a chest, chest, chest, He gave it to his niece, niece, niece.

Thumbs up, Un - cle Tom, Thumbs up, Un - cle Tom, Thumbs up,

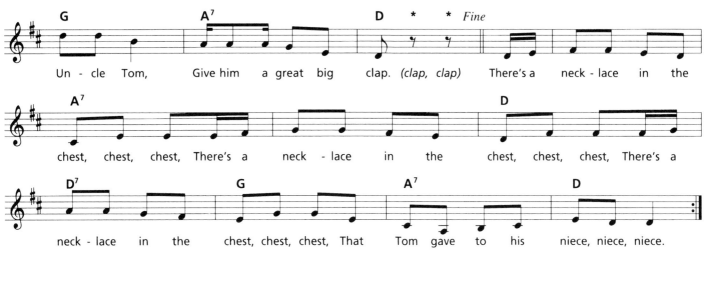

Un - cle Tom, Give him a great big clap. *(clap, clap)* There's a neck - lace in the

chest, chest, chest, There's a neck - lace in the chest, chest, chest, There's a

neck - lace in the chest, chest, chest, That Tom gave to his niece, niece, niece.

7 Bones

Words and music by Kaye Umansky

You've got to have bones to *(clap)* Hang your bo - dy on, Got to have bones to

(clap) Hang your bo - dy on, Got to have bones to hang your bo - dy on,

That's what bones are for. If you did - n't have bones to

(clap) Hang your bo - dy on, Did - n't have bones to *(clap)* Hang your bo - dy on,

Did - n't have bones to hang your bo - dy on, You'd be a big blob of jel - ly on the floor!

8 Body sense

Words and music by Ana Sanderson

I spy with my lit-tle eye, I hear with my lit-tle ear. A smell goes
up my nose, And I taste with my tongue which I hide in here, I taste with my tongue in
here. But I can feel all o-ver The whole of my
bo-dy, I can feel all o-ver: I can feel on my head, I can
feel on my nose; I can feel with my fin-gers And my toes.

9 What can you see?

Words and music by Sue Nicholls

What can you see? What can you see? I can see the pat-tern of the waves on the sea.

10 Here's a quiz

Words and music by Jane Sebba

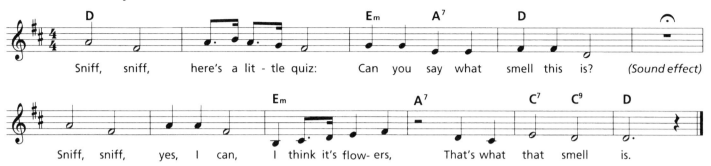

Sniff, sniff, here's a lit - tle quiz: Can you say what smell this is? *(Sound effect)*

Sniff, sniff, yes, I can, I think it's flow- ers, That's what that smell is.

11 Sweet potato

Traditional, adapted by Ana Sanderson

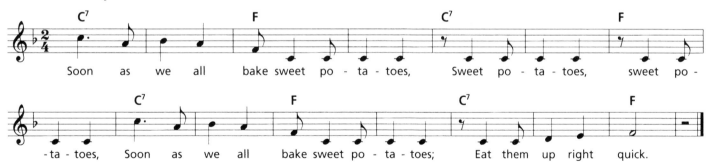

Soon as we all bake sweet po - ta - toes, Sweet po - ta - toes, sweet po -

-ta - toes, Soon as we all bake sweet po - ta - toes; Eat them up right quick.

12 I'm so hot

Words and music by David Moses

I'm so hot, it's no joke, I could drink a whole can of Coke.

I'm so hot, ev-en in the shade, I would love a li-tre of le-mon-ade.

I'm so hot, I should think I need a bu-cket of pink, fiz-zy drink.

I'm so hot, think I ought-a Be a-ble to fi-nish up a bath full of wa-ter.

I'm so hot, I could take A swim-ming pool full of va-nil-la milk-shake.

I'm so hot, I have a no-tion I could swal-low the At-lan-tic O-cean.

14 Jelly belly

Words and music adapted by P. Tresize

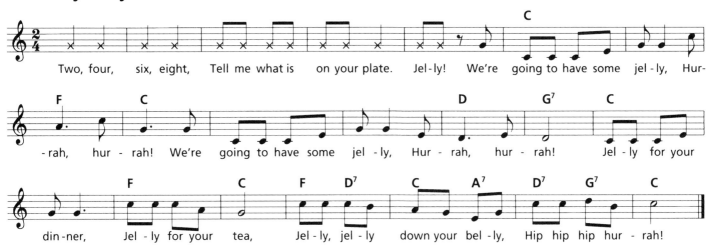

Two, four, six, eight, Tell me what is on your plate. Jel-ly! We're going to have some jel-ly, Hur-rah, hur-rah! We're going to have some jel-ly, Hur-rah, hur-rah! Jel-ly for your din-ner, Jel-ly for your tea, Jel-ly, jel-ly down your bel-ly, Hip hip hip hur-rah!

16 Too big for my boots

Words and music by Ana Sanderson

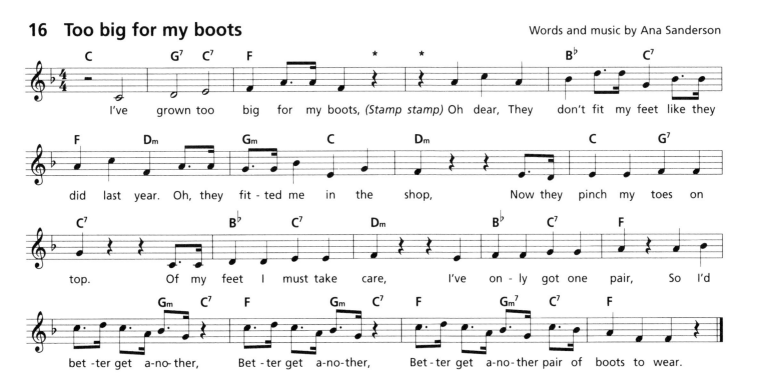

I've grown too big for my boots, (Stamp stamp) Oh dear, They don't fit my feet like they did last year. Oh, they fit-ted me in the shop, Now they pinch my toes on top. Of my feet I must take care, I've on-ly got one pair, So I'd bet-ter get a-no-ther, Bet-ter get a-no-ther, Bet-ter get a-no-ther pair of boots to wear.

17 Going over the sea

Traditional, adapted by Ana Sanderson

When I was one I had some fun, The day I went to sea.____ I jumped a-board a sail - ing ship, And the cap - tain said to me, 'I'm go - ing this way, that way, For-wards and back - wards, O - ver the deep, blue sea.____ A bot - tle of rum to fill my tum, That's the life for me.'

18 All I want for Christmas (is my two front teeth)

Words and music by Don Gardner

19 I love to laugh

Words and music by Richard M Sherman and Robert B Sherman

I love to laugh, Ha! Ha! Ha! Ha! Loud and long and clear.___ I

love to laugh, Ho! Ho! Ho! Ho! It's get-ting worse ev-'ry year.___ The

more I laugh, Ha! Ha! Ha! Ha! The more I fill with glee.___ And the

more the glee, Hee! Hee! Hee! Hee! The more I'm a mer-ri-er Me! Ha! Ha!

Me! Ho! Ho! Me! It's em-bar-ras-sing! The more I'm a mer-ri-er me!___

20 Very, very sad

Words and music by David Moses

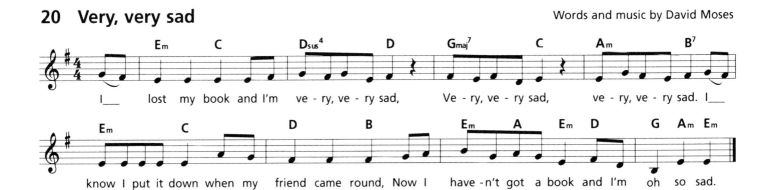

I___ lost my book and I'm ve-ry, ve-ry sad, Ve-ry, ve-ry sad, ve-ry, ve-ry sad. I___

know I put it down when my friend came round, Now I have-n't got a book and I'm oh so sad.

21 Doctor, Doctor

Words and music by David Moses

Doc - tor, Doc - tor, help me do, I feel a lit - tle sick and I don't want to.

Give me a pow - der, give me a pill. Hur - ry, hur - ry, Doc - tor, 'cause I do feel ill.

22 Me? I'm great!

Words and music by Jane Sebba

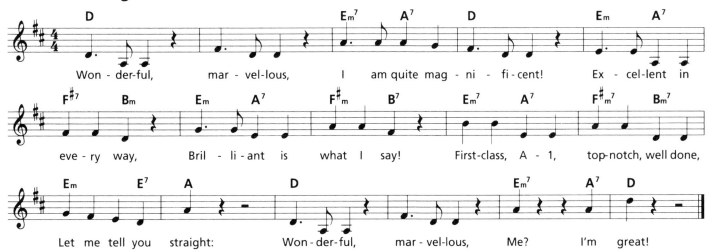

Won - der - ful, mar - vel - lous, I am quite mag - ni - fi - cent! Ex - cel - lent in

eve - ry way, Bril - li - ant is what I say! First-class, A - 1, top-notch, well done,

Let me tell you straight: Won - der - ful, mar - vel - lous, Me? I'm great!

Index of song titles and first lines

Acknowledgements

The following have kindly granted their permission for the reprinting of copyright material:

18 All I want for Christmas (is my two front teeth) Words and Music by Donald Gardner © 1947 Witmark-M-Sons, B. Feldman & Co Ltd, London W8 5SW. Reproduced by permission of International Music Publications Ltd (a trading name of Faber Music Ltd. All Rights Reserved.

19 I love to laugh Words and Music by Richard Sherman and Robert Sherman © 1964 Wonderland Music Company Inc, USA, Warner/Chappell Artemis Music Ltd, London W6 8BS. Reproduced by permission of Faber Music Ltd. All Rights Reserved.

Jill Darby for 5 Hair, © Jill Darby

David Moses for the words and music of 12 I'm not so hot, 20 Very, very sad and 21 Doctor, doctor © David Moses

Sue Nicholls for the words and music of 9 What can you see? © Sue Nicholls, A&C Black Publishers Ltd.

6 Uncle Tom from 'Sounds Topical' by Jan Holdstock © Oxford University Press 1995. All Rights Reserved.

Leon Rosselson for 4 You need skin © Leon Rosselson.

Ana Sanderson for 8 Body sense, 16 Too big for my boots and 23 Mahachagogo © Ana Sanderson 1997, A&C Black Publishers Ltd.

Jane Sebba for 10 Here's a quiz, 13 Food wrap and 22 Me? I'm great © Jane Sebba 1997, A&C Black Publishers Ltd.

The Singing Kettle for 14 Jelly belly. Courtesy of Cilla Fisher of the Singing Kettle.

Kaye Umansky for 7 Bones © Kaye Umansky 1997, A&C Black Publishers Ltd.

Every effort has been made to trace and acknowledge copyright owners. If any right has been omitted, the publishers offer their apologies and will rectify this in subsequent editions following notification.

The compiler and publishers would also like to thank the following people who have generously assisted in the preparation of this book and recording: James Fagan, Maureen Hanke, Helen MacGregor, Nancy Kerr, Sandra Kerr, Sue Nicholls, Sheena Roberts, Jane Sebba, Michelle Simpson, Marie Tomlinson, Jane Tootell and John Whiting.